Christmas Carols
for ACCORDION

ARRANGED BY GARY MEISNER

2   Away in a Manger

4   Bring a Torch, Jeannette, Isabella

6   Deck the Hall

8   The First Noël

10   Go, Tell It on the Mountain

12   Good King Wenceslas

14   Hark! The Herald Angels Sing

16   The Holly and the Ivy

18   I Heard the Bells on Christmas Day

20   It Came Upon the Midnight Clear

22   Jingle Bells

24   Jolly Old St. Nicholas

26   Joy to the World

28   March of the Toys

7   O Christmas Tree

32   O Come, All Ye Faithful (Adeste Fideles)

34   O Come, Little Children

48   O Little Town of Bethlehem

36   Silent Night

38   Toyland

40   Up on the Housetop

42   We Three Kings of Orient Are

44   We Wish You a Merry Christmas

46   What Child Is This?

ISBN-13: 978-1-4234-3177-0

HAL•LEONARD®
CORPORATION

7777 W. BLUEMOUND RD. P.O. BOX 13819 MILWAUKEE, WI 53213

In Australia Contact:
Hal Leonard Australia Pty. Ltd.
4 Lentara Court
Cheltenham, Victoria, 3192 Australia
Email: ausadmin@halleonard.com

Visit Hal Leonard Online at
www.halleonard.com

AWAY IN A MANGER

Traditional
Words by JOHN T. McFARLAND (v.3)
Music by JAMES R. MURRAY

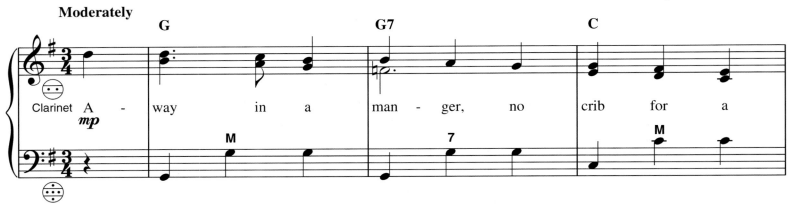

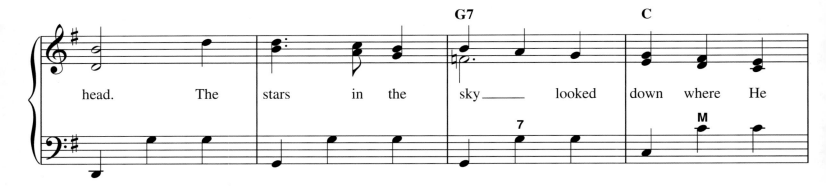

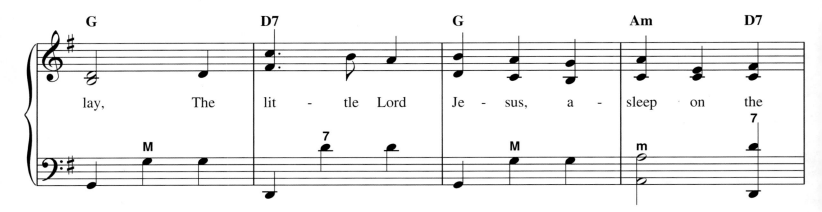

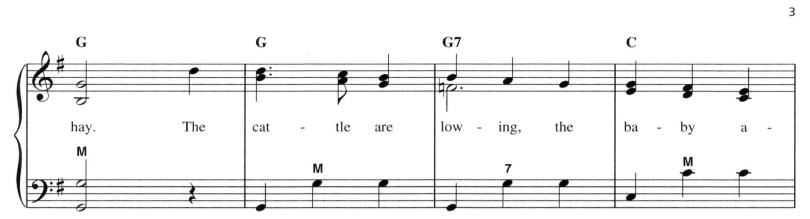

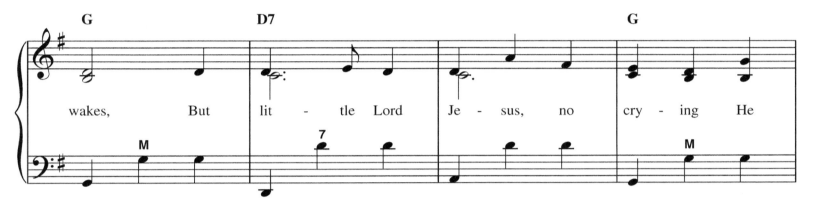

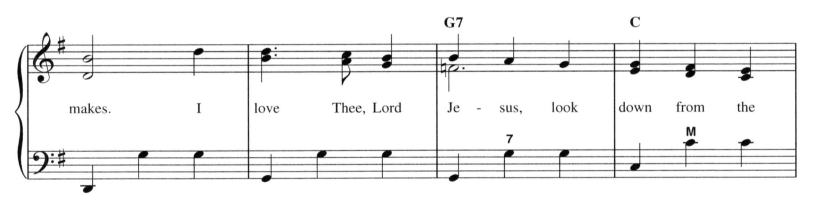

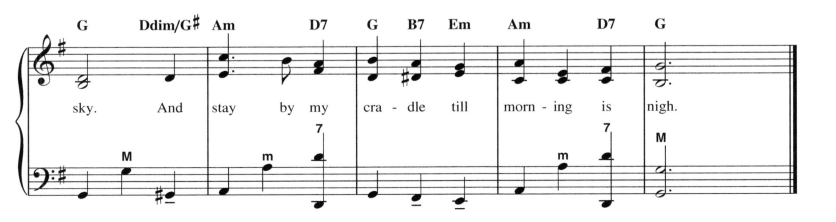

BRING A TORCH, JEANNETTE, ISABELLA

17th Century French Provençal Carol

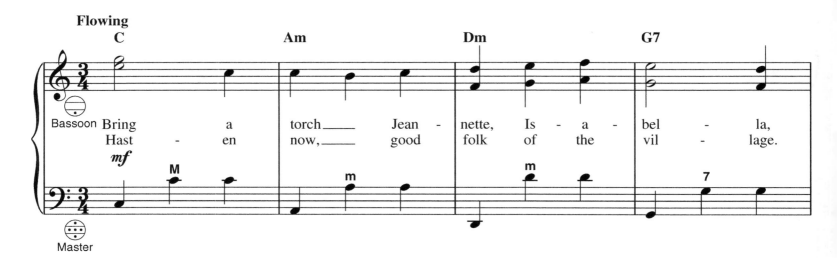

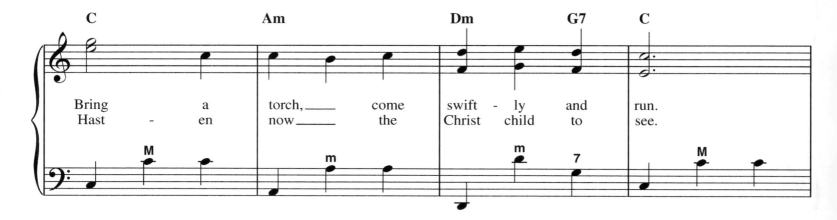

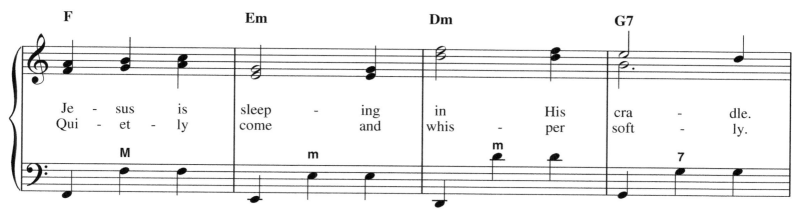

DECK THE HALL

Traditional Welsh Carol

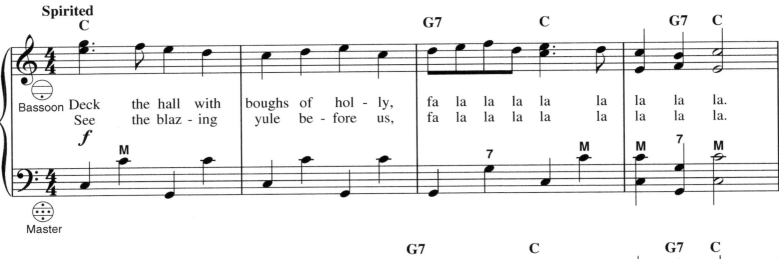

Bassoon
Deck the hall with boughs of hol-ly, fa la la la la la la la la.
See the blaz-ing yule be-fore us, fa la la la la la la la la.

Master

'Tis the sea-son to be jol-ly, fa la la la la la la la la.
Strike the harp and join the chor-us, fa la la la la la la la la.

Don we now our gay ap-par-el, fa___ la fa___ la la la la.
Fol-low me in mer-ry meas-ure, fa___ la fa___ la la la la.

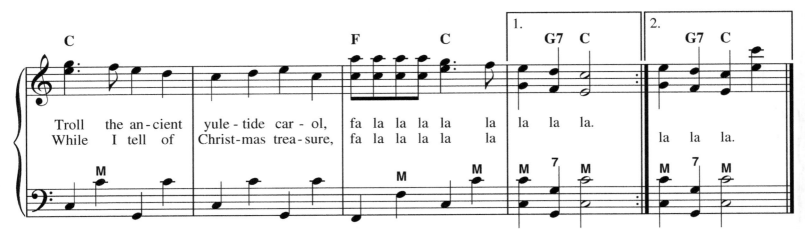

Troll the an-cient yule-tide car-ol, fa la la la la la la la la.
While I tell of Christ-mas trea-sure, fa la la la la la

1.
la la la.

2.
la la la.

O CHRISTMAS TREE

Traditional German Carol

THE FIRST NOËL

17th Century English Carol
Music from W. Sandys' *Christmas Carols*

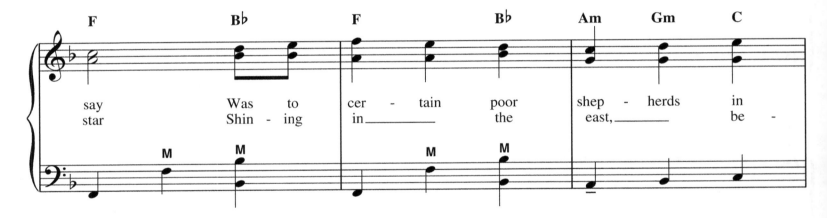

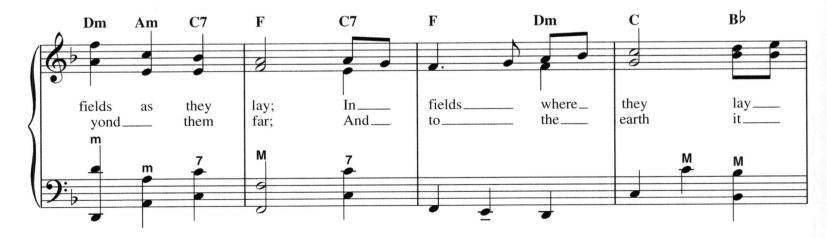

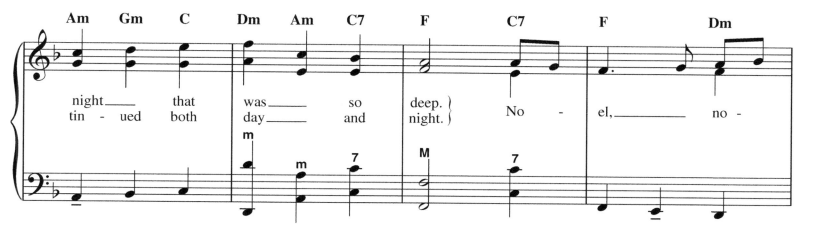

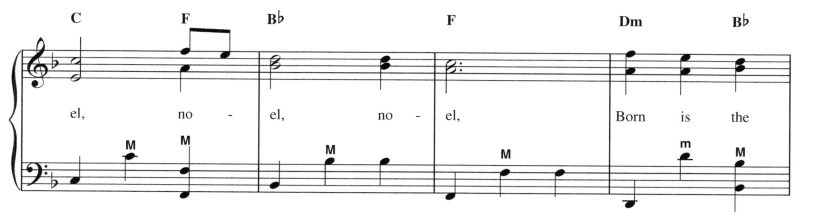

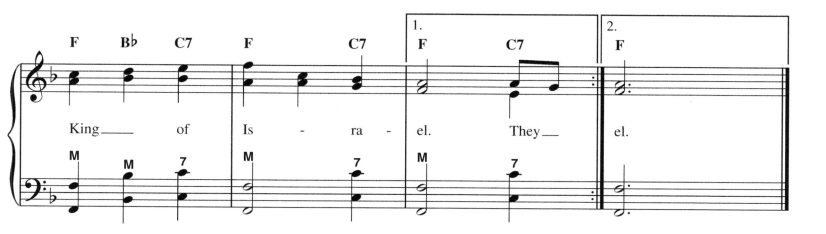

GO, TELL IT ON THE MOUNTAIN

African-American Spiritual
Verses by JOHN W. WORK, JR.

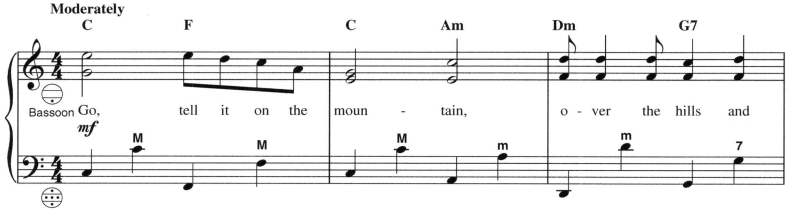

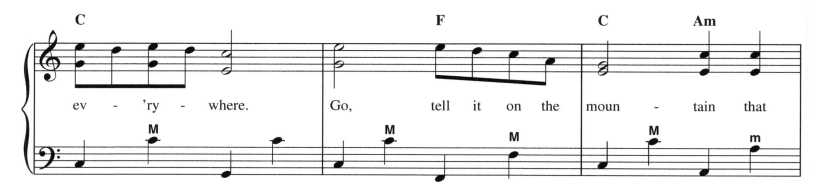

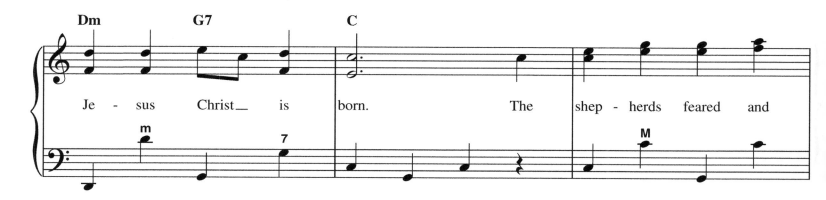

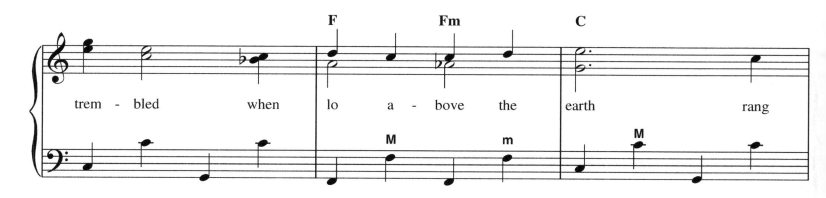

out the an - gel cho - rus that hailed our Sav - ior's

birth._____ Go, tell it on the moun - tain,

o - ver the hills and ev - 'ry - where. Go, tell it on the

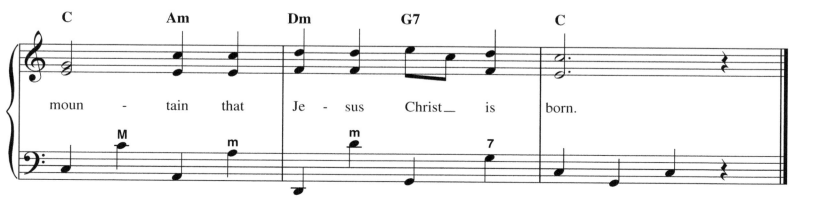

moun - tain that Je - sus Christ_ is born.

GOOD KING WENCESLAS

Words by JOHN M. NEALE
Music from *Piae Cantiones*

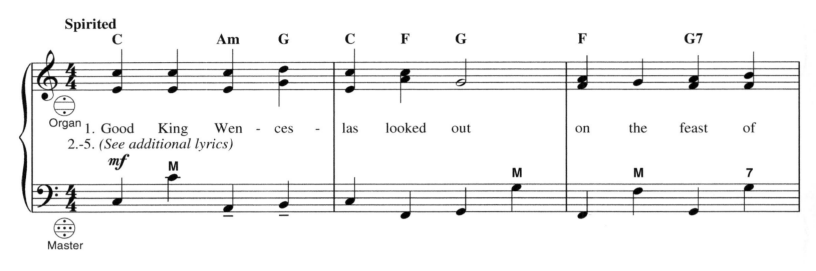

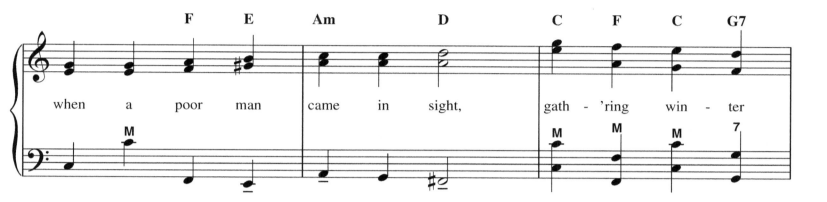

Additional Lyrics

2. "Hither page, and stand by me,
   If thou know'st it, telling,
   Yonder peasant, who is he?
   Where and what his dwelling?"
   "Sire, he lives a good league hence,
   Underneath the mountain;
   Right against the forest fence,
   By Saint Agnes' fountain."

4. "Sire, the night is darker now,
   And the wind blows stronger;
   Fails my heart, I know not how,
   I can go no longer."
   "Mark my footsteps, my good page,
   Tread thou in them boldly:
   Thou shalt find the winter's rage
   Freeze thy blood less coldly."

3. "Bring me flesh, and bring me wine,
   Bring me pine-logs hither;
   Thou and I will see him dine,
   When we bear them thither."
   Page and monarch forth they went,
   Forth they went together;
   Through the rude winds wild lament:
   And the bitter weather.

5. In his master's steps he trod,
   Where the snow lay dinted;
   Heat was in the very sod
   Which the saint had printed.
   Therefore, Christian men, be sure,
   Wealth or rank possessing,
   Ye who now will bless the poor,
   Shall yourselves find blessing.

HARK! THE HERALD ANGELS SING

Words by CHARLES WESLEY
Altered by GEORGE WHITEFIELD
Music by FELIX MENDELSSOHN-BARTHOLDY
Arranged by WILLIAM H. CUMMINGS

Moderately

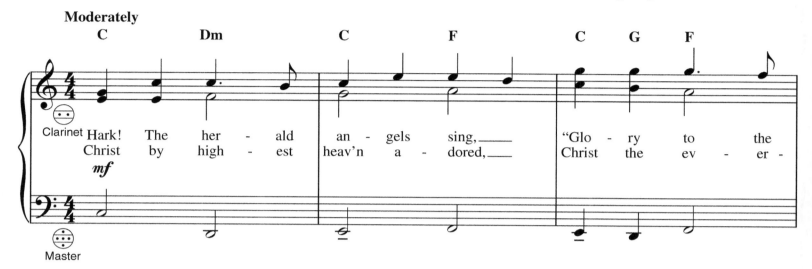

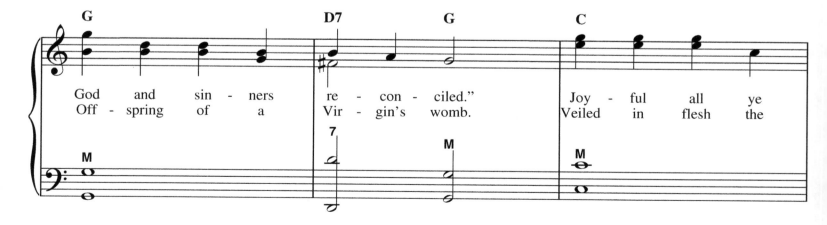

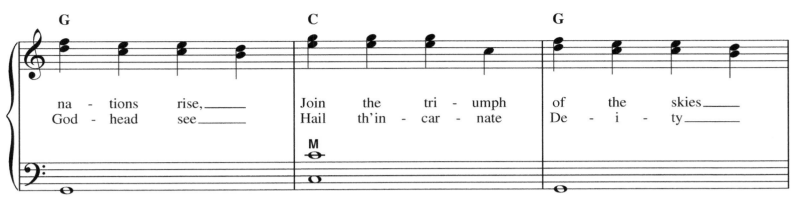

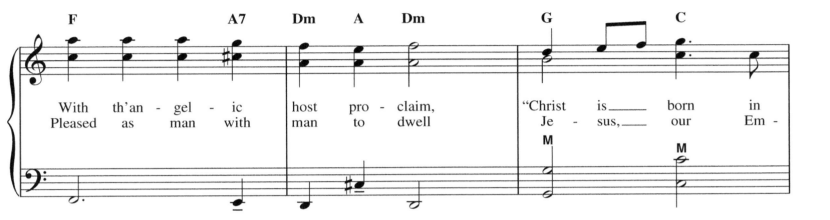

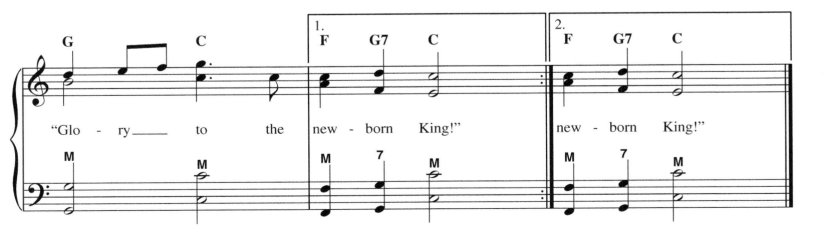

THE HOLLY AND THE IVY

18th Century English Carol

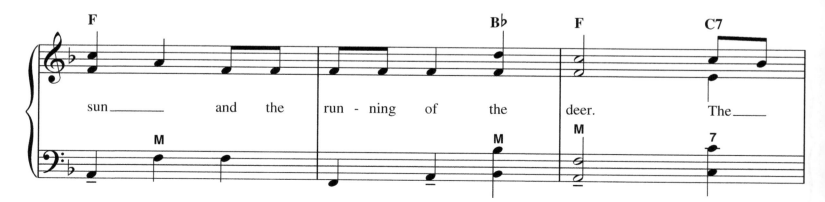

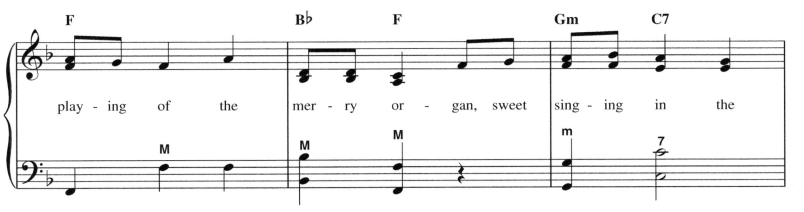

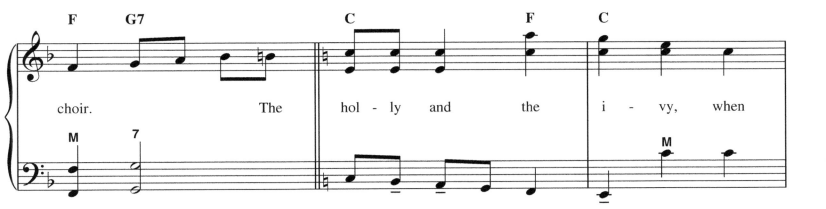

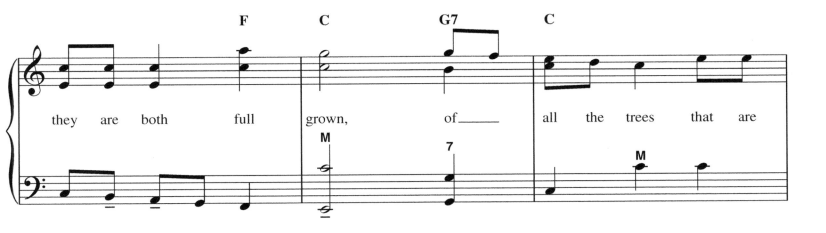

I HEARD THE BELLS ON CHRISTMAS DAY

Words by HENRY WADSWORTH LONGFELLOW
Music by JOHN BAPTISTE CALKIN

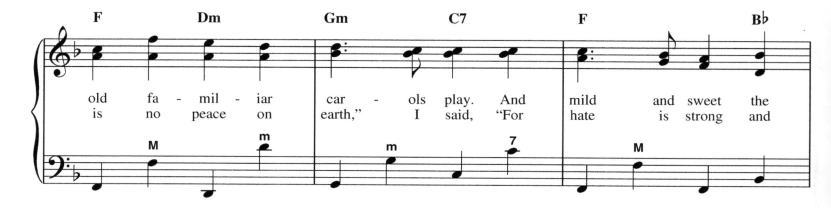

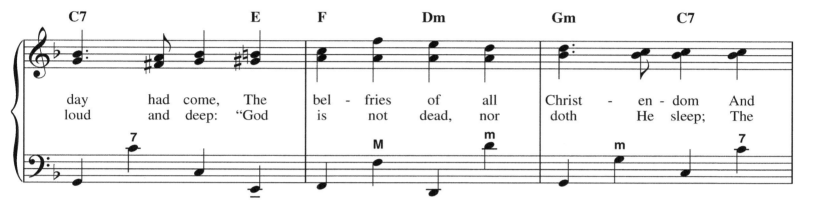

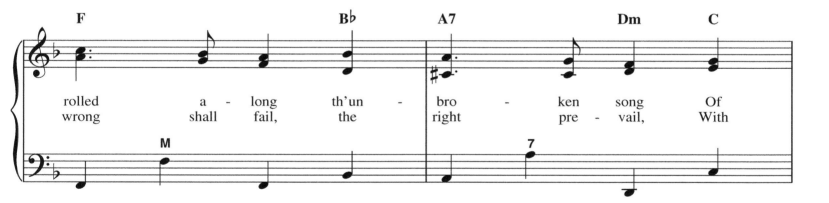

IT CAME UPON THE MIDNIGHT CLEAR

Words by EDMUND HAMILTON SEARS
Music by RICHARD STORRS WILLIS

Slowly

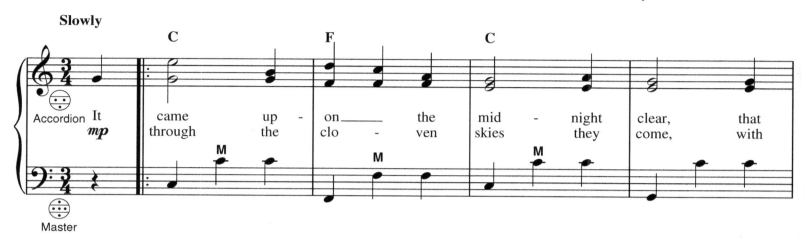

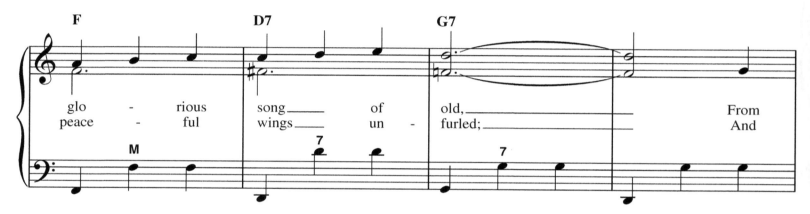

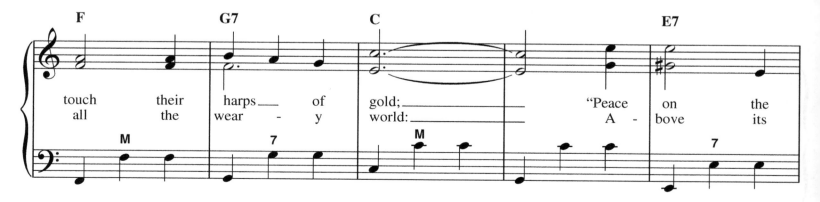

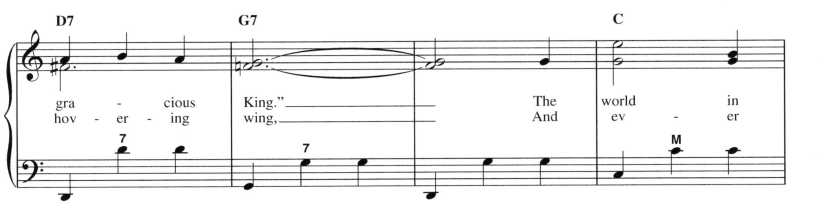

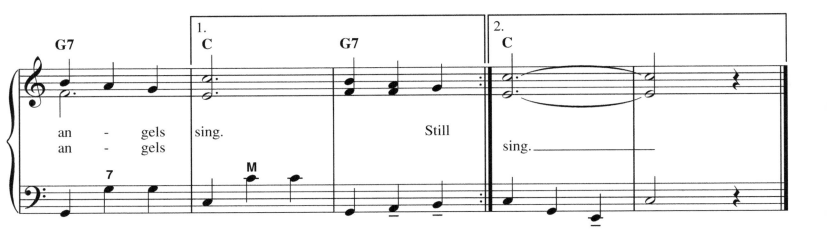

JINGLE BELLS

Words and Music by
J. PIERPONT

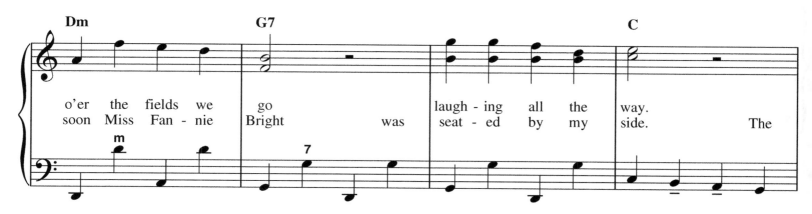

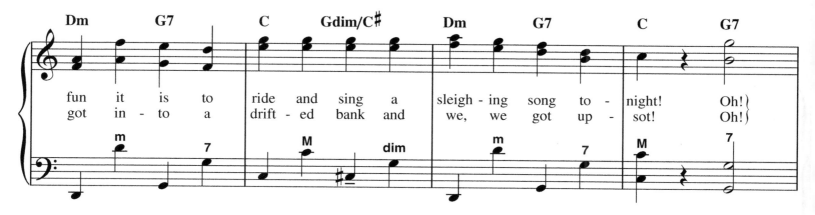

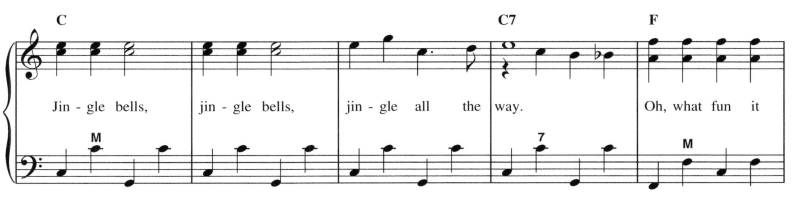

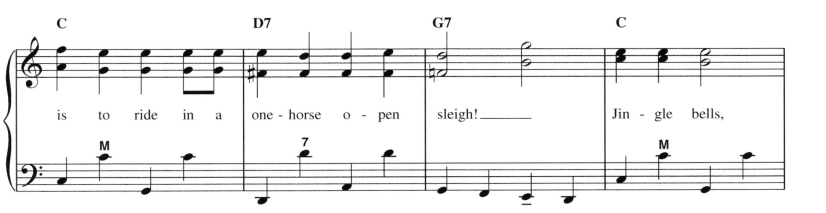

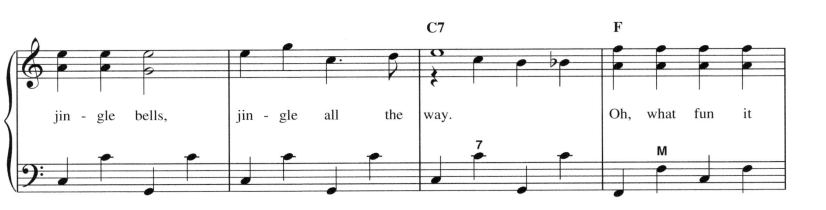

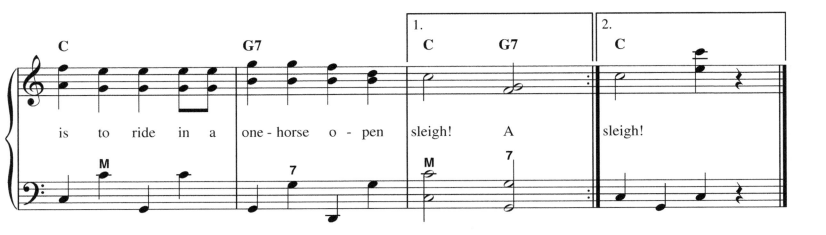

JOLLY OLD ST. NICHOLAS

Traditional 19th Century American Carol

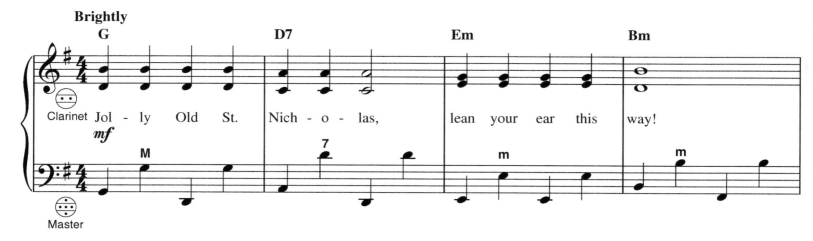

Jol - ly Old St. Nich - o - las, lean your ear this way!

Don't you tell a sin - gle soul what I'm going to say.

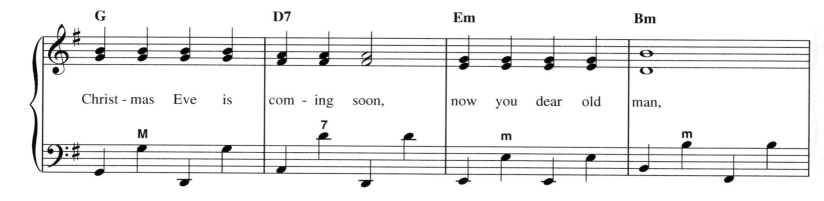

Christ - mas Eve is com - ing soon, now you dear old man,

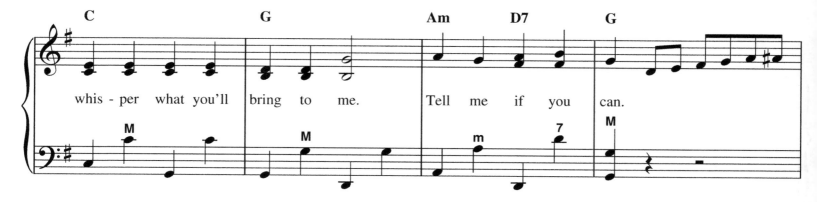

whis - per what you'll bring to me. Tell me if you can.

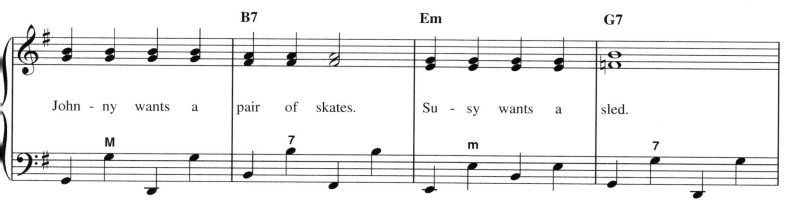

Johnny wants a pair of skates. Susy wants a sled.

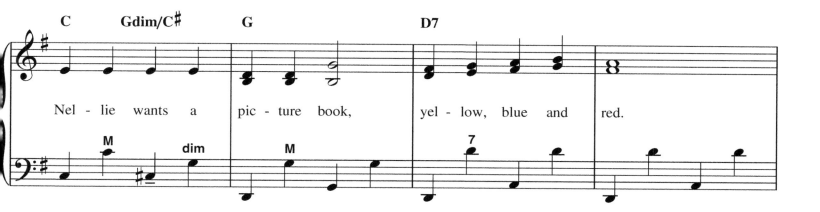

Nellie wants a picture book, yellow, blue and red.

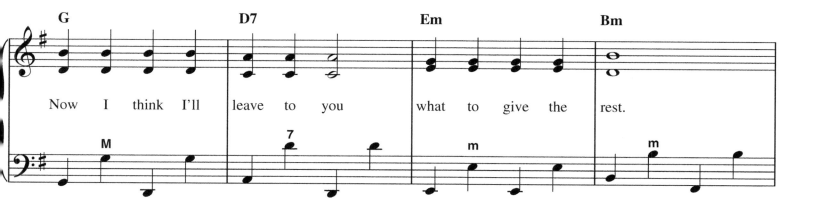

Now I think I'll leave to you what to give the rest.

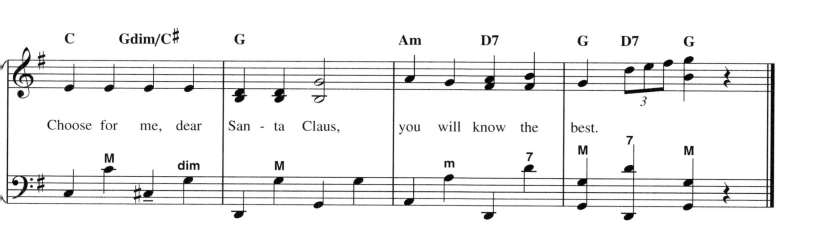

Choose for me, dear Santa Claus, you will know the best.

JOY TO THE WORLD

Words by ISAAC WATTS
Music by GEORGE FRIDERIC HANDEL
Arranged by LOWELL MASON

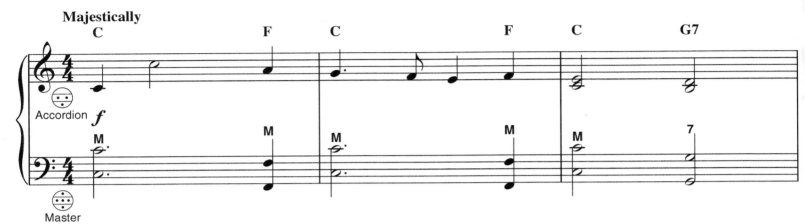

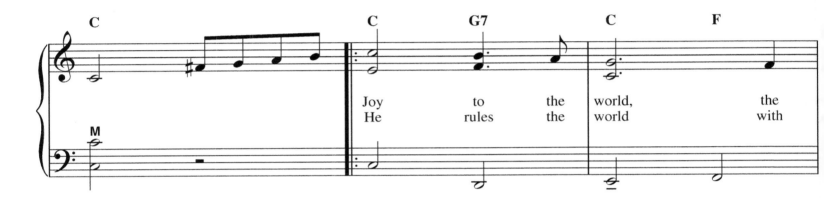

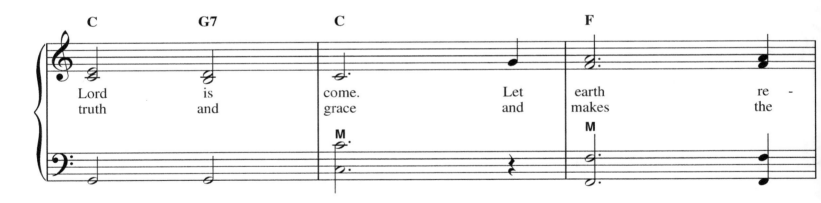

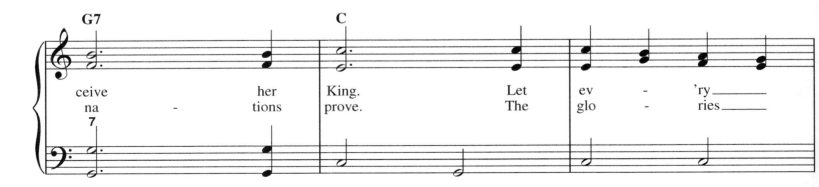

heart _____ pre - pare _____ Him _____ room, _____ And
of _____ His right - eous - ness, _____ And

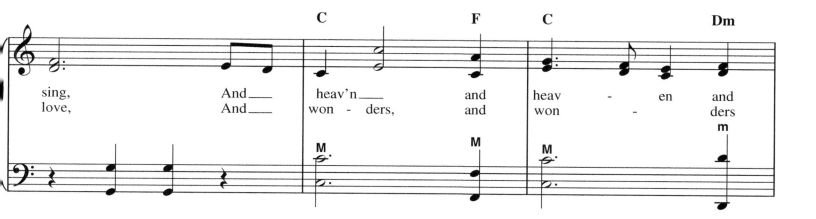

G7

heav'n and na - ture ___ sing, And ___ heav'n and na - ture ___
won - ders of His ___ love, And ___ won - ders of His ___

C F C Dm

sing, And ___ heav'n ___ and heav - en and
love, And ___ won - ders, and won - ders

C G7 1. C 2. C

na - ture sing. love.
of His

MARCH OF THE TOYS

By VICTOR HERBERT

March tempo

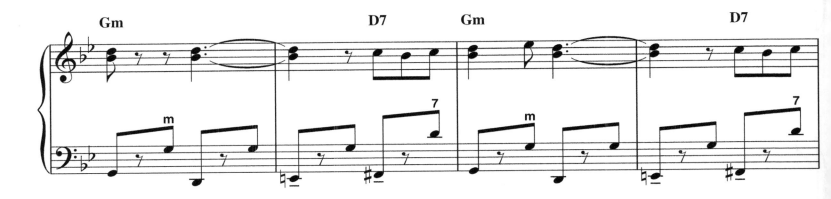

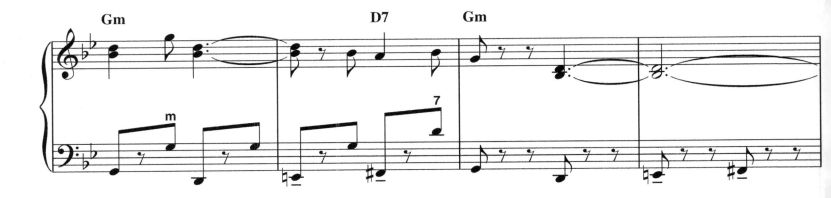

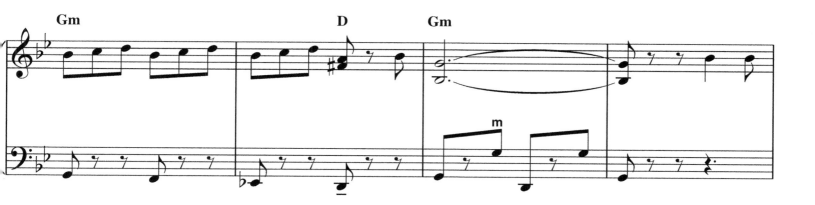

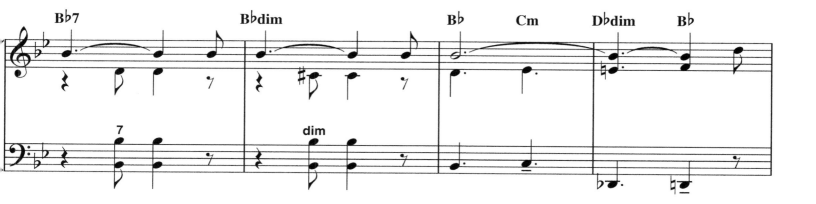

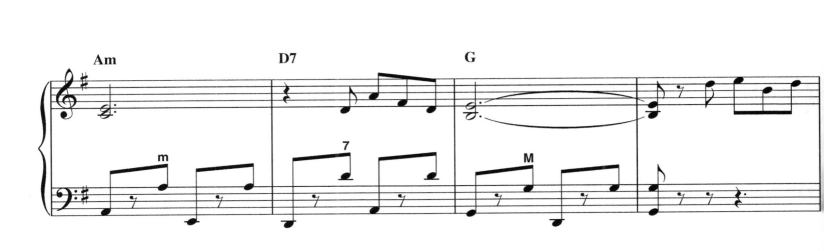

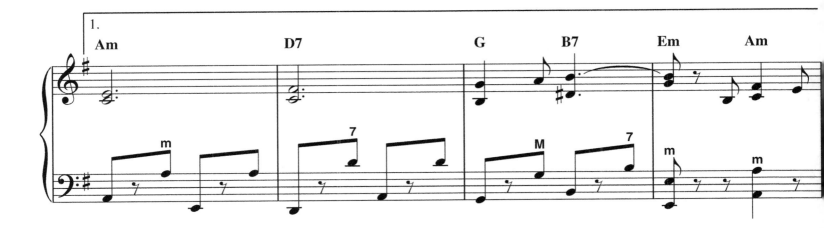

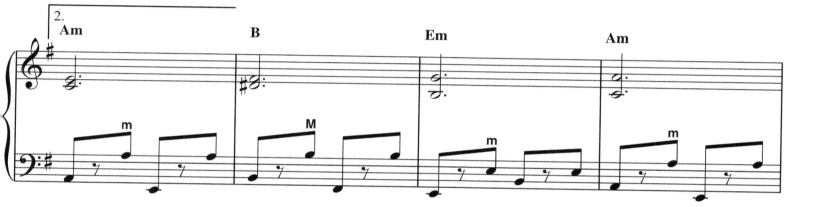

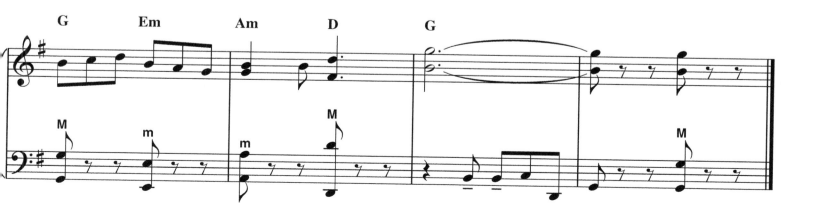

O COME, ALL YE FAITHFUL
(Adeste Fideles)

Words and Music by JOHN FRANCIS WADE
Latin Words translated by FREDERICK OAKELEY

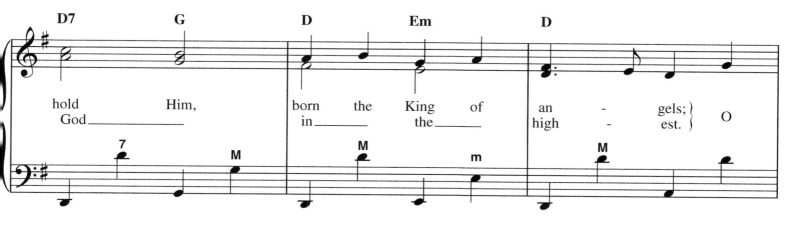

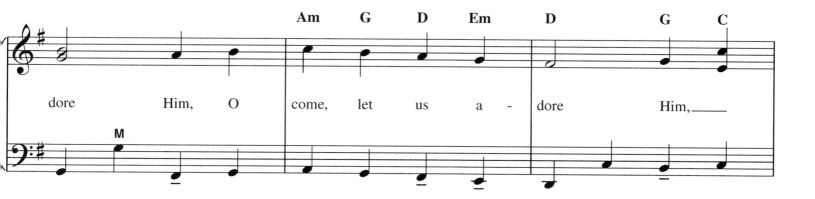

O COME, LITTLE CHILDREN

Words by C. VON SCHMIDT
Music by J.P.A. SCHULZ

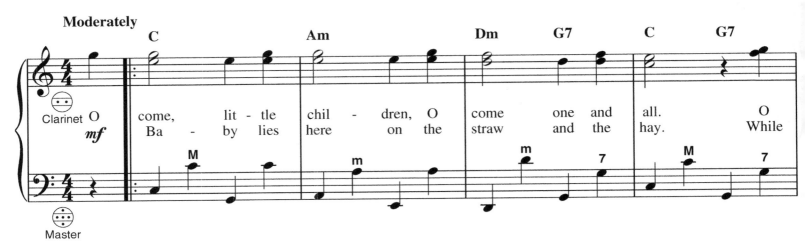

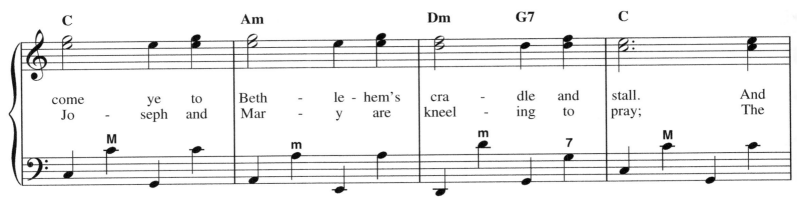

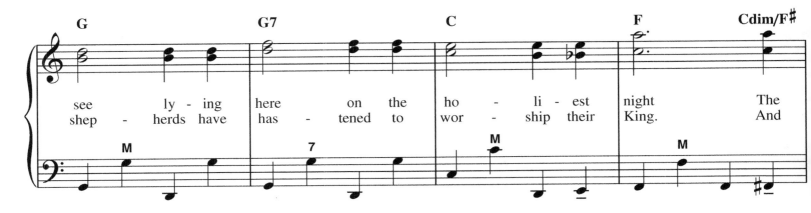

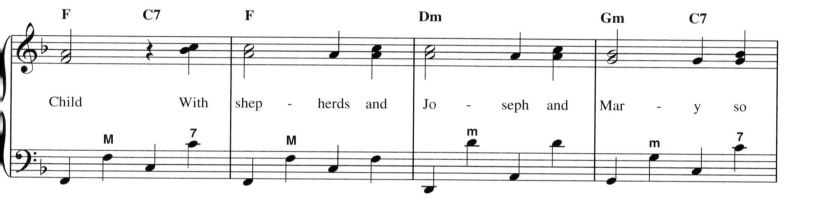

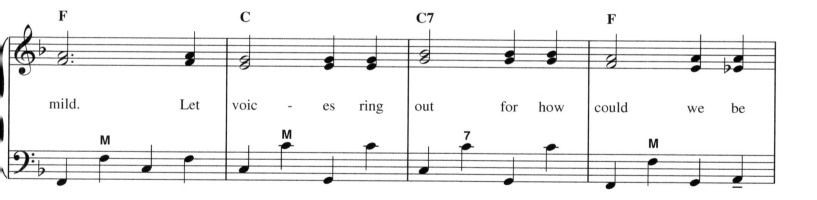

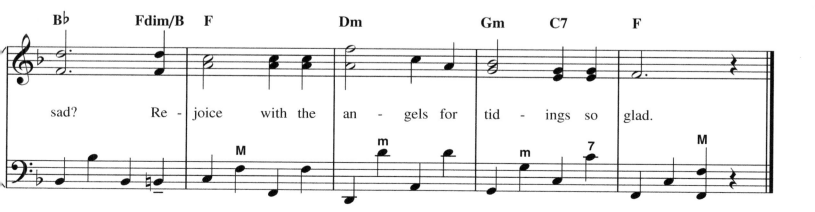

SILENT NIGHT

Words by JOSEPH MOHR
Translated by JOHN F. YOUNG
Music by FRANZ X. GRUBER

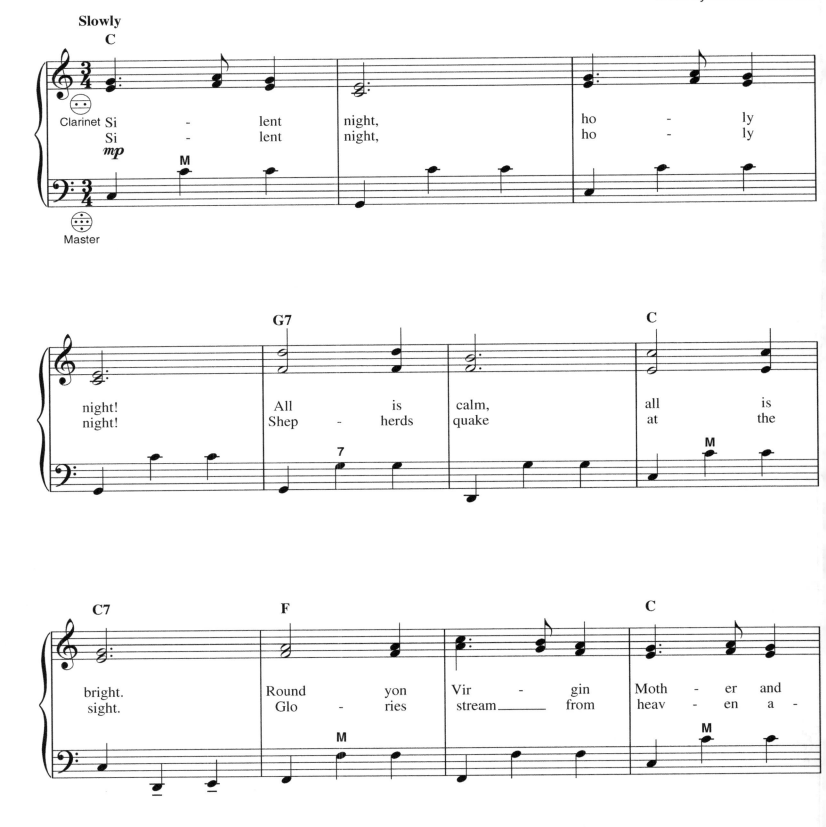

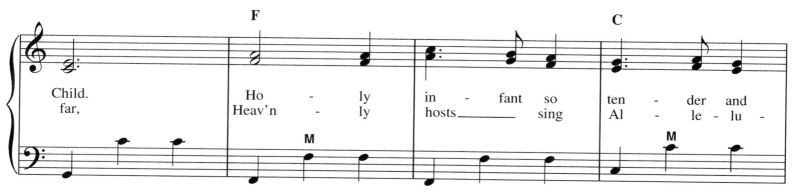

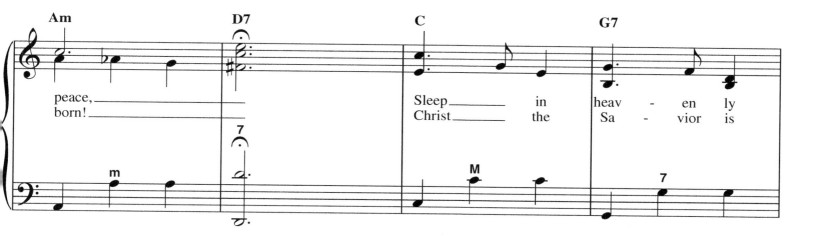

TOYLAND

Words by GLEN MacDONOUGH
Music by VICTOR HERBERT

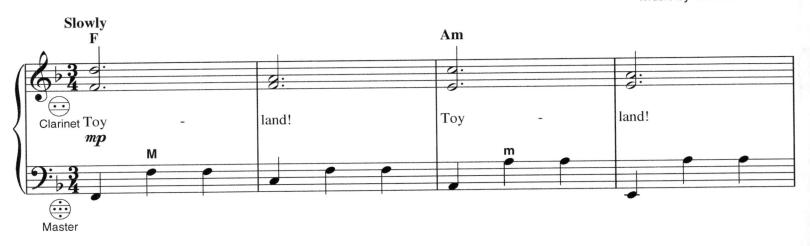

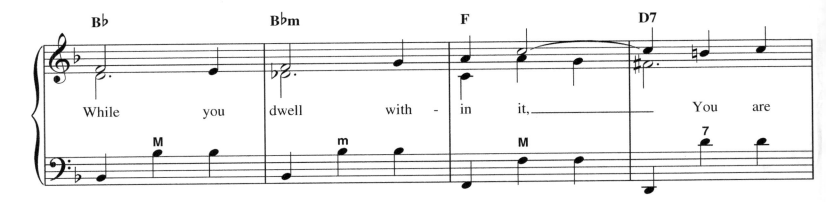

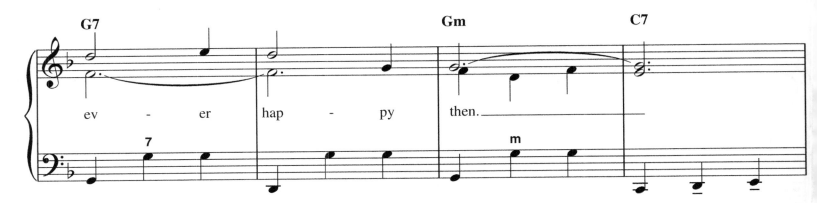

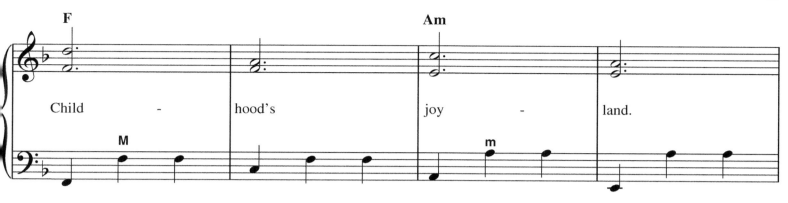

Child - hood's joy - land.

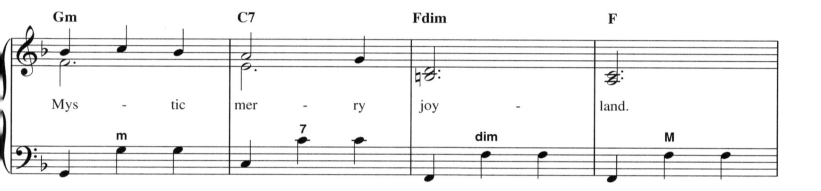

Mys - tic mer - ry joy - land.

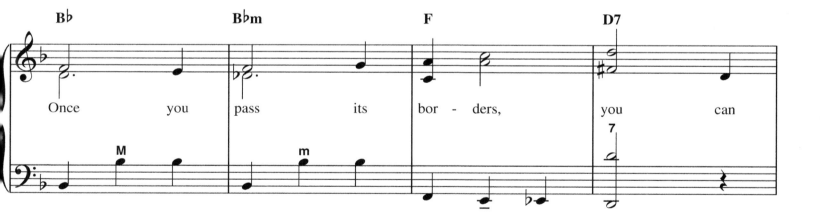

Once you pass its bor - ders, you can

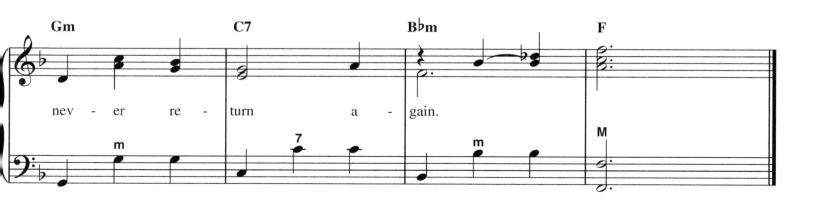

nev - er re - turn a - gain.

UP ON THE HOUSETOP

Words and Music by
B.R. HANBY

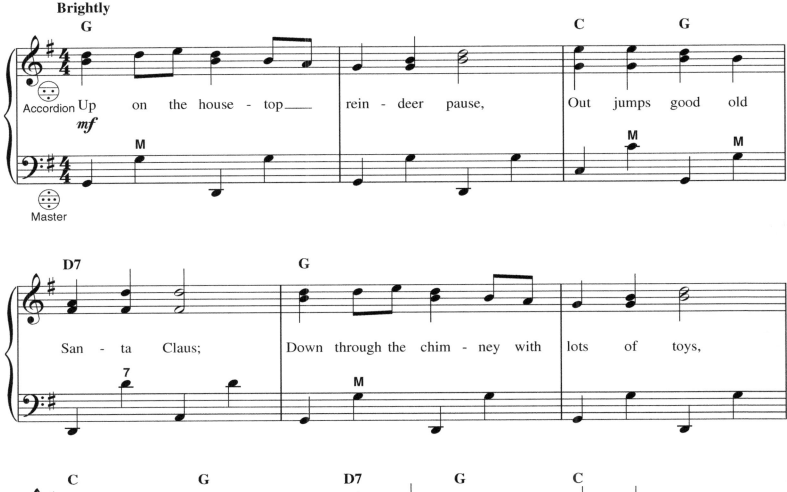

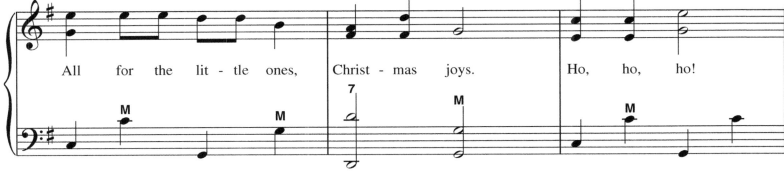

WE THREE KINGS OF ORIENT ARE

Words and Music by
JOHN H. HOPKINS, JR.

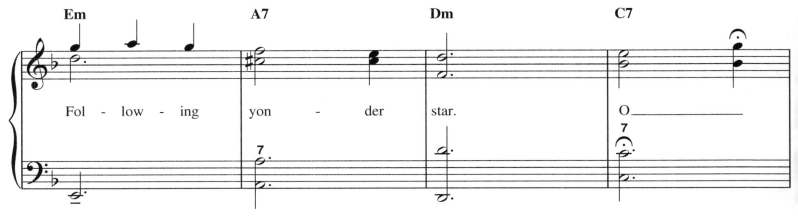

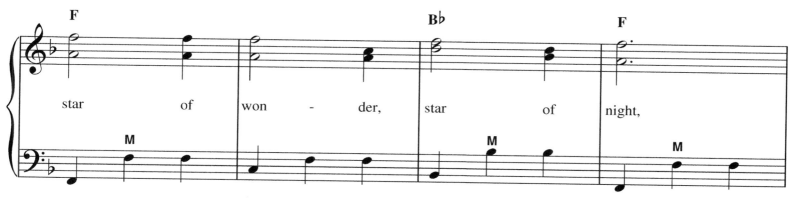

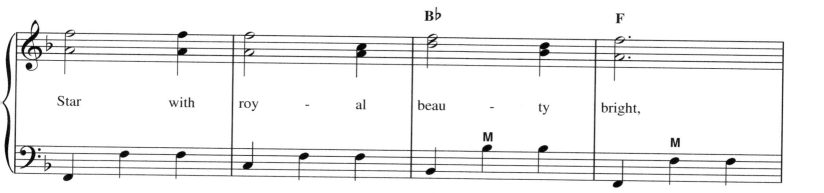

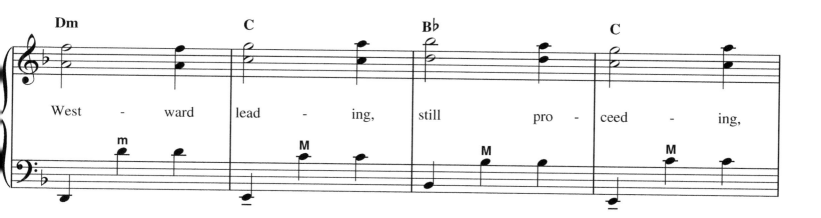

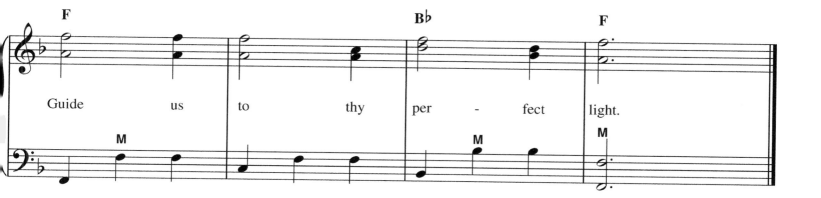

WE WISH YOU A MERRY CHRISTMAS

Traditional English Folksong

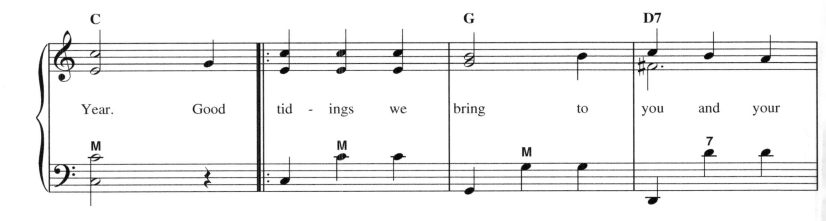

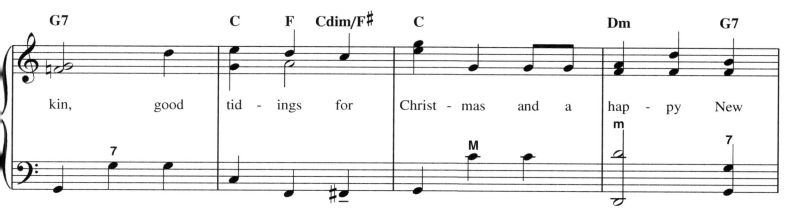

WHAT CHILD IS THIS?

Words by WILLIAM C. DIX
16th Century English Melody

Slowly

Bassoon *mf*

Master

What Child is this, who, laid to rest, On
bring Him in - cense, gold and myrrh, Come

Mar - y's lap is sleep - ing? Whom an - gels
peas - ant king to own Him; The an King of

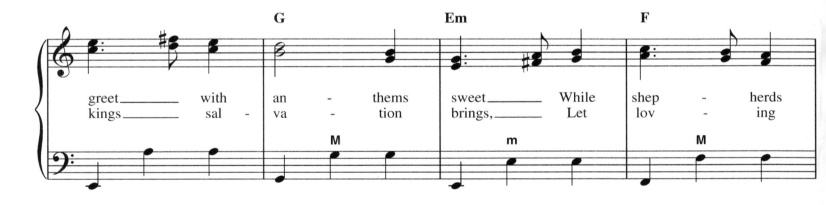

greet with an - thems sweet While shep - herds
kings sal - va - tion brings, Let lov - ing

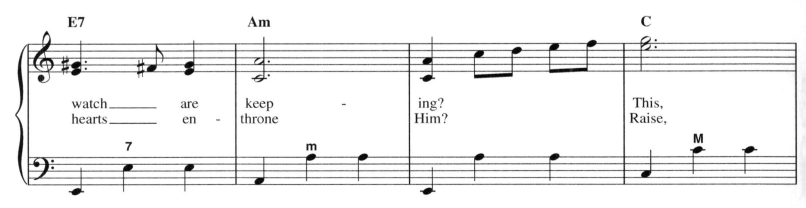

watch are keep - ing? This,
hearts en - throne Him? Raise,

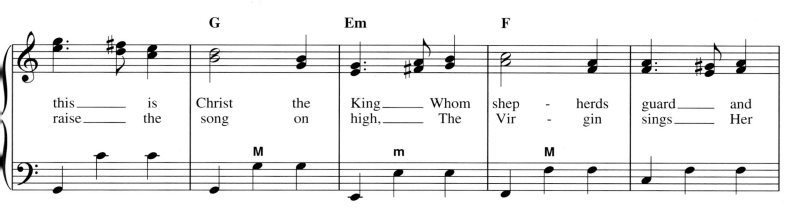

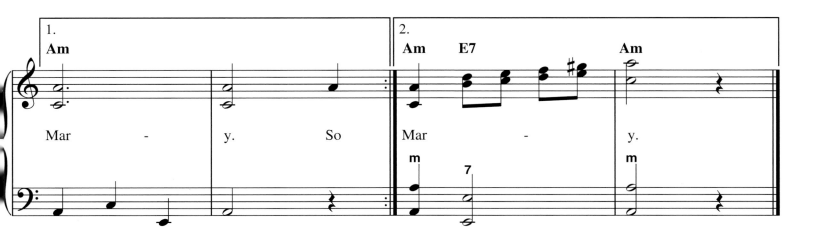

O LITTLE TOWN OF BETHLEHEM

Words by PHILLIPS BROOKS
Music by LEWIS H. REDNER

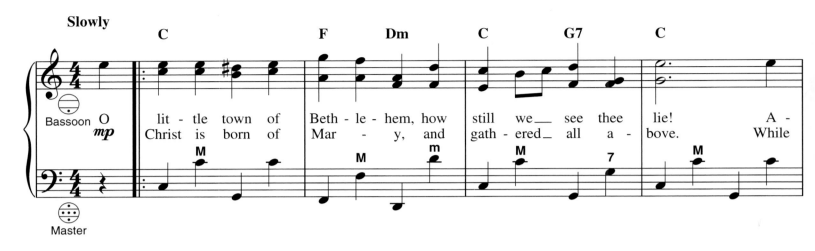

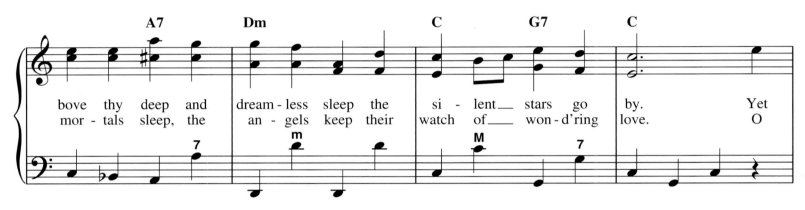

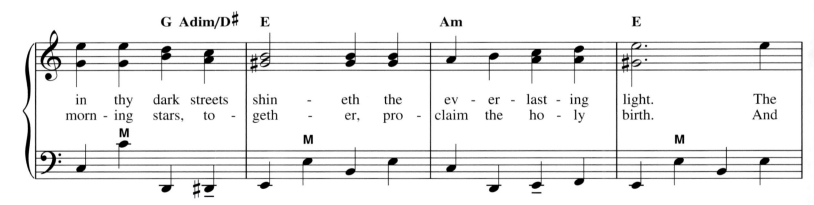

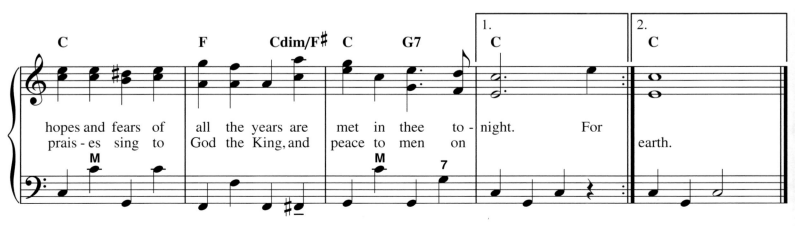